white spaces where we learn to breathe

by Murgatroyd Monaghan

Off Topic Publishing

First print edition: August 2025 by Off Topic Publishing

Copyright © Murgatroyd Monaghan, 2025

All rights reserved. No part of this publication may be reproduced, stored or transmitted in any form or by any means, electronic, mechanical, photocopying, recording, scanning, or otherwise without written permission from the publisher. It is illegal to copy this book, post it to a website, or distribute it by any other means without written permission, except for brief passages quoted in a review.

NO AI TRAINING: Without in any way limiting the author's and the publisher's exclusive rights under copyright, any use of this publication to "train" generative artificial intelligence (AI) technologies to generate text is expressly prohibited. The author reserves all rights to license uses of this work for generative AI training and development of machine learning language models.

Paperback ISBN: 978-1-7389885-4-9

eBook ISBN: 978-1-7389885-5-6

Front Cover Design: Murgatroyd Monaghan

Design and Layout: Marion Lougheed

Off Topic Publishing: www.offtopicpublishing.com

Praise for
white spaces where we learn to breathe

white spaces where we learn to breathe precisely and compassionately unearths the humanity of experiences long denied the agency of a storytelling voice in the mainstream. Murgatroyd Monaghan has crafted a gripping collection of works that are both tender and fierce, making space for lives and stories that deserve every medium of expression. This book is a comforting embrace and a rallying cry.

> **— Waubgeshig Rice, *Moon of the Crusted Snow*, recipient of the Debwewin Citation for excellence in First Nations Storytelling**

This collection left me gutted, moved, and deeply grateful. These poems don't just tell stories. They insist on being witnessed. Each one reaches back into history and forward into the present, refusing separation between the personal and the political, the intimate and the inherited. They mourn lives stolen and shortened, hold space for mothers who bleed and daughters who breathe through fear, and call out injustice with a voice that is clear, unsparing, and necessary.

What struck me most is how these poems carry their grief and their fire side by side. The writing is fierce, yes, but it's also deeply tender. There's a kind of love here — for community, for truth, for the act of surviving — that runs beneath every line.

Reading this work, I felt anger, sorrow, recognition, and a quiet sense of responsibility. These are poems that won't let you look away. They ask something of you. And they stay with you long after the final word. This is the kind of poet whose voice doesn't just linger, it transforms you.

> **— Chanel Sutherland, winner of the 2025 Commonwealth Short Story Prize, the CBC Short Story Prize and the CBC Nonfiction Prize**

This collection is a deeply-felt, deeply moving reflection on the colonial project and its impact upon Black and Indigenous peoples (as well as the Scots.) Like all the best poets, Monaghan makes incisive observations with a few devastating and memorable words. In dedicating many of the poems to individuals who were murdered by police and/or mistreated by the justice system, the reader is invited to do further research, thus increasing the impact and importance of these poems beyond their pages. The inventive use of language, punctuation and space introduces a playful quality that reminds us to seek joy even in the face of suffering; in this way, Monaghan's poems beautifully affirm our common humanity and connectedness.

As I read, I found myself not so much forgetting to breathe as exhaling in recognition. There is a picture of lungs on the cover, but this book is about our hearts.

— **Zilla Jones, *The World So Wide*, winner of the Journey Prize**

white spaces where we learn to breathe's political assertiveness, and its desire to mirror back colonialism's linguistic debt, offer coverage for a text that—at its heart—is really about care. Care for others, care for words, care built into the formation of the life that serves as background (and occasional subject) for its poems. Murgatroyd Monaghan's experimentalist ethic is really a best-case scenario for contemporary poetry: it is there to make you see the invisible. She is there to make you care for the invisible.

— **Jacob McArthur Mooney, *Folk*, Trillium Book Award shortlist**

Exquisite in their resistance and playfully irreverent, these poems from Murgatroyd Monaghan breathe beautiful, complicated, and messy life."

— **Hollay Ghadery, award-winning author of *FUSE***

A forceful rhythmic collection of poems full of heart and hunger—for space, justice, respect, love, recognition, and tenderness. It is an invitation to dwell in spaces that Murgatroyd has carved out for us so we can listen to the multilayered, polyvocal score sung by the voices she has, as if by magic and with deep abiding tenderness, brought to the page, her own included. Her poems enfold and uphold—through language and form—those who have been erased and buried by colonial, ableist, misogynist, racist, market, and circumstantial pressures. They push against the edges both literally and figuratively, deftly playing with and subverting literary and language conventions as an intentional act of resistance, using the page as a weapon against oppression and erasure. The white spaces in the title and in the collection act as both breath and knee, leading us the readers, right to the brink—forcing us to leap past our willful insistence on rules to risk awakening. And it is a risk well worth it. An invitation to listen to English without the red tape—"a lang-a-wichdatmaiks / kommunsents!" to "keep looking together togethertogether" so "we can melt it with our tears."

> — **Nancy Huggett, winner of the 2024 RBC PEN Canada New Voices Award**

A visually stunning work of art both poignant and relevant [that] reminds me of the beauty and strength that exists within the human spirit. It was a pleasure to read.

> — **Joseph Kakwinokanasum,** *My Indian Summer,* **winner of the First Nations Communities READ Award**

Praise for Murgatroyd Monaghan

"By bringing together a handful of individuals who have little in common beyond the fact that they occupy the same rail passenger car as it sets out from Toronto and travels through boreal forest and onto the plains, "The Train" shows how quickly a makeshift but caring community can be built from scratch. These individuals, who've only just met each other, are all dealing with their own private troubles and crises — including one especially dramatic and immediate crisis. A series of finely tuned scenes shows how they open up to and look after each other in spontaneous and tangible ways."

— **Leona Theis, Short Grain Contest 2023 judge**
Grain Magazine

"A touching story that is effective in its use of understated prose."

— **Brianna Cheng, Off Topic Contest Judge on Honourable Mention "Bean"**

"A compelling story about motherhood and growing up. The descriptions are incredibly vivid, and the story is captivating."

— **Lindsay Foran, Off Topic Contest Judge, on Honourable Mention "Bean"**

"Murgatroyd Monaghan's "Thumbs," hooked me with its evocative imagery, and tenderness for fish kin. [...] The poem oscillates between human and fish perspective, deploying unexpected metaphors of nation, asylum, and language, an affective, empathetic work complicating the binary of human and animal."

— **Mercedes Eng, 2023 Pacific Spirit Poetry Prize judge,** *Prism*

"'The Train'" unfolds a story of strangers on a train who find unlikely ways to bond over their various experiences of sadness and death, with the narrator's children igniting interactions and sparking connections in ways only children can. The children are brilliant, the dialogue crisp, the character development deftly handled. The piece cleverly incorporates the best techniques of fiction into creative nonfiction to reveal a true storyteller's voice. Bravo."

— **Lisa Bird-Wilson, 2024 CNF Contest judge**
Creative Nonfiction Collective

"An incredible piece filled with rich language, visuals and depth."

— **Carolyn Parsons, Off Topic Contest Judge on Honourable Mention "Autopsy of a Tongue"**

For all of us.

Dear reader,

white spaces where we learn to breathe is art that combines space, text and punctuation as social commentary on both the spaces that are typically "white spaces," and also the spaces left behind by missing and murdered BIPOC on Turtle Island. The reader is encouraged to breathe inside these spaces, and to observe them as one might observe a moment of silence. The text itself is an insertion into white space, that of the page. As with all dark skin in white spaces, the text can feel awkward and uncomfortable to the colonized in terms of its placement on the page or the way it interrupts your thoughts or flow. *white spaces* exists to ask the white reader to sit and breathe with this discomfort, while celebrating the experiences of BIPOC, who are used to breathing in spaces that are not made for them, and for whom we must ensure safer spaces, where something that white folks often take for granted — simply *breathing* — feels joyous and natural.

Some poems are written to honour specific Black and Indigenous persons who lived courageously and died in white spaces, and in the case of missing or murdered BIPOC, specific white space will be provided for your consideration, while other poems reflect or explore themes of existing within white space. All of these poems are the result of lived experience combined with hundreds of hours of research and connection and introspection, including scrutinizing my own privilege.

Punctuation and spelling are strongly colonial constructs which have been made to exclude BIPOC from white-dominated spaces, such as academia and literature, whilst patois and cants have been created and used by oppressed peoples to express themselves within their newfound context; a way to not just bend rules, but also to hide in plain sight. These broken rules are beautiful actions of resistance, a whole new language of growth and revolt against complacency during times of genocide, slavery and injustice. Some of the poems in white spaces challenge and break rules of spelling and grammar in an effort to celebrate this linguistic legacy, to preserve it, normalize it, and also to stretch the mind that has been trained to recognize colonial constructs of grammar and spelling as the only or best way to express oneself, be understood, or be published. Other poems focus on sounds, voice; some of the devices used in these poems include word play, rhythm and rhyme, which were used heavily by Inuit and other Indigenous Peoples and which Black people on this land pioneered through arts such as slam and cypher.

As oppressed persons have always done, each poem in "white spaces" uses all the tools at its disposal — every comma, every space, every line, every hyphen, every parenthesis, every consonant and vowel sound, every syllable — to advance its own freedom and life and purpose.

The arc of the poems is designed to flow in a way that helps readers to question their own thoughts and feelings of superiority, belonging and purpose using language, punctuation, and white space as tools as they ask themselves, what is poetry, what is language, and who designed my ideas about this?

I hope that you read these poems slowly, and that we all work hard to become more aware of the space we hold around us, the spaces we create, and the spaces we should leave for others.

With love,

Murgatroyd

table of contents

1	/	when she stopped flowing
3	/	2 (poems)
4	/	this minute has 22 hours
		(for waneek horn-miller)
5	/	they keep asking me…
8	/	overdue
15	/	protect them
17	/	storytellers
18	/	white spaces where we learn to breathe
19	/	freetung
20	/	roots
21	/	my mother calls my hair a bird's nest like it is an insult
23	/	star/light/tours
27	/	built on bones
33	/	a true story of 2 suicidal men in scar-borough
35	/	indiginnocent (for donald marshall jr.)
37	/	high as home, selling our souls to buy belonging

38	/	sometimes ,
39	/	island tongue
41	/	song for [caged] birds (for angela cardinal)
43	/	family portrait
44	/	the gardener
45	/	you think autistic people cannot be journalists because we suffer from black-and-white thinking
47	/	little blue blanket (after ritahester)
49	/	the ballad of mrs. g (for donna george)
52	/	have you ?
53	/	full circle
55	/	white knuckles/blacklists
57	/	driving
59	/	red herring
63	/	aftermath
64	/	blindness
71	/	About the Author

when she stopped flowing

anishinaabekwe; biigizawinaagozi
and as (still) as a *shimmering*echoechoecho

come, sting your palms on this ice:
the same ice has bruised her ( ) mother's knees.

maaminonenim! each snowflake on your sleeve
is different -   wipe your eyeseyeseyes

your nose, your spit, your slates
clean; wipe -   snowdust from this

fro-zen circle. everythingisconnected.
mikaw! keep looking. together togethertogether

we can melt it with our tears.

the following page is blank for our MMIGW2S.

2   (poems)

1   **rods and cones**   **(and hearts and bones)**

        the eye   (interprets the blue sky)
        and i   (see rainbows when you lie)

2   **brains and veins**   **(and love and pain)**

        light fools us again   (so high)
        my pretty fetty desperado -   (don't   die)

this minute has 22 hours
                        (for   waneek horn-miller)

                -    and you could not be safe
in death -   the bones
        of your ancestors having been desecrated in order
to make more space for a   golf course
                that nobody needed.

(pulsating, ripples of pain
        and endorphins,fat collecting on
the surface: memories of   intergenerational
wounds
        you carried before you
even knew the word for such a wound in your own tongue
                and both   official languages.

your dead roused that day, undormant -
        perhaps they are the ones
who held you then, prolonging your life for those22 hours.)

ancestors aside,
                22 hours is how long you bled, detained in
        dirt, unattended, while
                you   waited for care.

        i have heard the rude complaints of   white folks
waiting in the ER for only 2 hours.

"what the hell iswrong with theseguys, eh?" as they flip
through their magazines,making jovial chatter and heading
out every 15 minutes to pair their tim's with their cheap
reservation smokes

i want to display your brave face in every ER in the country –
        "see?! you colonizers areentitled to nothing.
                        go play   golf!"

they keep asking me…

why i stay (1) (since you asked)

i am brave to choose:

open wounds
        (if i prefer them to scars)
dying on my own land
        (over a new life on foreign soil)

                                      if i want to.

why i stay (2) (wait - you asking me again?)

i'll choose my heartbreak like i choose my eggs

today over-hard

tomorrow all scrambled

and next week, maybe i'll get that sunny side up.

yeah, i'm allergic to eggs, but i like eggs dammit and i carry an epi-pen in my pocket.

why i stay (3) (do i stutter????)

i'm an adult.

i want the eggs.

i ordered the damn eggs.

just let me eat my eggs in peace

and we can still smile together over breakfast.

why i stay (4) (in case you were allergic to my first answers)

blame the artists. the poets. the musicians. i can't tell poignant from poisonous; pain from passion; breakfast from breaking faster. i understood allergies in acrylic and anaphylaxis only as a blank page. someone cut my leg off and wrote a poem about the blood. i cried from the healing and learned to hop everywhere. someone played music one day and i fell in love. just like that. i never learned how to starve. i lick sugar off my calloused fingers, my scabby knees, his dirty toes, and i regret nothing. blame the artists, the artists, the freakin' artists.

why i stay (5) (   )

it's my brushstroke

it's my dissonance

it's my metaphor

it's mine

overdue

(small spaces where we don't breathe at all)

the average gestation period of the typical ontario youth custody facility is 36 days and i am overdue.

bloodied and blinded by daylight and the sudden freedom of my limbs, i sever my cord reluctantly.

i uncurl my palm to receive my shoelaces and iam handed a paper craft and a drawing i made of a tiger.

i am going to keep this picture and this craft and this baby but i am not sure about the shoelaces.

my entire happy childhood has taken place during my five and a half months in jail in northern ontario.

in retrospect, incarceration prepares me for prospective motherhood more than any prenatal class.

the life inside of me, and i, the life inside this punitive womb: we kick and kick until we are expelled,

like miseducation, a doo wop with no hill, innoculation with no shot, just shoot, kill.

we're a nation of new palpitations, from slaves on plantations, to ghettoization,

to coming of age behind bars and lactation like – damn. everything is wet. everything is new. everything hurts my eyes.

my feet land softly; a mother is not concrete, is not bars, and
survival rations suffice in wartime.

for this child, it will always be wartime.

this autumn day i am released but not reborn; my initials stay
etched into a steel uterine lining.

though scraped from the pink flesh of my hollow insides, the
child inside me has a home, while i wander without shelter.

the cusp of winter and my jumpsuit itches but the clothes i
was arrested in no longer fit my roundness.

i carry a near-empty garbage bag which i climb inside to sleep
and pray that we could all have wombs for landlords.

the paper cup craft sits open, begging for change, and i clutch
the tiger into the baby and me.

so don't think i didn't decorate that garbage bag nursery.

i stay awake and dream of what i will name this baby
though no one, no one, knows my name

(wide open spaces where some of us stop breathing)

it is twenty years on and i am a woman and not a tiger and
both my shoes have shoelaces. i straighten my kinky hair.

brown bodies sprawl over cold concrete like helpless ragdolls.
familiarity breeds common contempt for urban carnage.

junkies are basically earthworms draped over storefronts
left to fry and dry in the gentrified light of the sun.

if you think of it that way, others tell me, it gets easier.
 easier for who? i think.

but six months later i am stepping over these bodies
and i am thinking of starbucks coffee

or my kids' homework
or anything, anything that isn't death.

i don't know another way to do it.
i know this time that i am not designed for war.

i make sure bodies are breathing.
i make sure they're not alone.

socks turned inside out litter the tracks,
abandoned by addicts searching for veins

or trains
as if there is even a difference.

one foot and then the other;
a long journey either way.

everything in this landscape is
used up and then abandoned:

needles, lighters, condoms, courage

and me, ready to hand out more of all of the above.

tarpaulins draped across milk crates
face the grey sky unashamed.i am no tarpaulin.

tap taptaptaptaptap:
rain gathering on blue plastic;

calloused fingers summoning blue vessels;
skin and canvas waiting to give, to fall, to fail.

the white noise of storms and of bloodflow
are indistinguishable. pulsing, whooshing;

the embryonic comforts of a malignant opioid womb.
every line has blurred. my curls return in the rain.

yesterday morning the girl was here,
the one i keep remembering, the one who said,

"nothing has ever soothed me like this rain."
or maybe she said pain. it doesn't matter.

a train came between us and i was secretly relieved.
i pulled out my novel to quell my fears with fantasy,

to hide in a world i could leave without consequence
knowing dystopia is fiction and evil is conquered easily by
children with courage.

when the roar passed, i stepped over
the tracks. she was all the wrong colours.

i removed the tourniquet but
the blood did not return.

tonight, candles in cups flicker like eyelids,
bright flames dance like tiny pupils,

shadows twist off of her wounds like sterile water and darken
the sky
but still we do not know her name.

used up and abandoned.
used up and abandoned.

drip dripdripdripdrip:
wax collecting on flimsy plastic;

liquid spilling into cookers;
memory and memorial colliding.

today someone new is under the same tarp.
the turnover is quick.even the death camps here have wait
lists.

those who still know how to grieve are another species,
dissolving like delicate narcotic powders into their own sterile
tears,

stirred gently with a monogrammed silver spoon.
i shake my head and harden like wax.

who can afford to be fragile?
we burst like veins.

maybe i am too jaded to be relieved,
or maybe in war there is simply no time.

all i know is stepping over this body and moving on to the next

the next

    the next

  the next

(large and small spaces where the next generation and the child inside us both learn how to breathe)

the average gestation period of the sumatran tiger is twenty-six weeks.

unlike me, the tiger is a mother instinctively. she doesn't worry what kind of mother she will be.

she births tiny black-and-orange balls of fur whose main function is to always stay unseen.

a mother tiger teaches her young that it is safest to always slip between the cracks.

what she wants to tell them instead is, if you want to be a hippopotamus, or a crocodile, or anything tougher than what you are

i will cast any spell to make it so, and i will pay the witch doctor with my own life.

inside our garbage bag womb, my eyelids grow heavy and my tiger pries herself from her 2-dimensional prison.

perhaps she has served her time or is escaping or is dissolving from the caustic sound of her newborn child whimpering in fear.

reaching sympathetically through the bars of the page, she licks the tears from my wild mane,

the grime from my claws, and her roughness comforts me.

as one of her young now, she reminds me to stay out of sight. *there are many predators here*, she whispers.

but tiger mama, i whisper back, *how can a girl hide herself out here?*

tiger mama smiles at me with sharp teeth.

a girl cannot be safe, she says. *that is why all of my children become tigers.*

(breathe)

protect them

i'm not sure how we still keep liv-

ing while our ndnwomen are

                                          dead

but…

        (more than that)

…

i'm not sure how theystill keepdy-

ing while we are

                                          alive

the next page is blank for pondering unrhetorical questions

storytellers

      the moment our love was born

was when we reached out with gentle fingertips to stroke these strange, white borders

and with carefully weighted eyes, we asked,

    "how did you get that scar?"

and for the first time since arriving in this country, neither of us lied

                              about the answers.

      the moment our love was lost

was when you saw my blood had saturated every trash-can tissue

and I noticed your last fingernail had ( )disappeared

    between your angry teeth

and both of our hearts kept beating, even though we didn't

                              know the story.

white spaces where we learn to breathe

1. our first breaths are full of the scent of blood. puddled between our mother's legs, we, inhale and then cry out at the stench of her suffering. we, expel her sterile fluids from our lungs and nothing about us is ever pure again. we, do not apologize for flinging our limbs into more space than we've ever existed in ever before but still, we feel unsafe outside of the confines of a blanket swaddled flat, a cradle, a wrap. when we are one second old is when we realize that safety and freedom can never coexist.

2. we, never stop breathing never stop breathing never stop. (breathe.) breathing. our mothers are the air in our lungs and the blood between our legs. they, (breathe) spread out. salty sticky sick sans safety we, (breathe) choke. our mothers are a bone in our throats. the stains don't come out with any of the remedies she swore by. the homemade recipes for whitening women's shirts only work for the current generation. we, wear clothes that boast our mother's stains as well as ours and we, (breathe) ignore the pain. this town's air is thick with blood.

3. in pregnancy our bellies swell up like we are allergic to love. our babies take up the space we had for breathing, for bleeding, for being. we look in the mirror and don't recognize what we are seeing. we prepare to become the weapon rather than the wound. in our child's first moment we will open and she will fall into a pool of all our pent-up blood as sheinhales the scents of stains we can't ever tell her how to get clean. but at night, we, unwrap the blankets to let her limbs stretch out, free of every doubt, open up the window, whisper, what am i, what are you, what are we, what is safety anyway? (breathe -

freetung

    ingle shizthalang
        widgawev'thakull
   anneyezerz-heer
      ingle shizthawepp
  unnuhv'thakull
       anneyezastoomay
kyoofeelinfeereeyer
       ollwaischaynjin
  golltharoolztoo
      keeypyooinliyn.
  kullaneyezd'pee
    pulstrah gull tureed
 thisspakozzthayt
     raydidkommins
ensforsumthinkoll
      da nejookaysh
un. owpinnuhpiyu
    riyzandunlernit.
lerntroothaggen.
      taykthakolloniyz
erskoolroolzwee
    ollerndanjuss
 tuffthum
   !!!!!!!!!!!!!!!!!!!!!!!!!   !

roots

some people will not love you.

they will shame you for the soil beneath your fing-ernails

after asking you to dig your grave with your bare hands.

your labour was not a waste.

i suggest you plant an oak tree, in-stead

something strong, with roots that thrive six feet deep

and leaves that give their bodies repeatedly, for the good of the soil

that loves your fing-ernails so much.

my mother calls my hair a bird's nest like it is an insult

    - and now, in my thirties, i call you for the first time. i am sitting and you are tugging at my nest and i can't breathe. your brown fingers swish-swish switch-switch handle the hair god gave me into cornrows which he didn't. these first braids are my first look at a Black father who didn't stay. i don't cry out when it hurts. these will stay four weeks you tell me; maybe less cause my hair is so thin. fragile blonde kinky electrified neglected like my heart. like my heart. light and wild and beautiful.

cornrows into puffs, i said. you said, 160$. i sent you
my deposit then sat there guilty for three days. i felt like
i had bought something illegal.

    bird's eye view: all these braids criss-crossing over such straight lines. you make it look graceful; planned. my mother never planned me. i don't look how i thought i would look with braids. i can't remember if i thought i'd look Blacker or whiter. but i still look like me. i feel disappointed, and then disappointed in myself for feeling that way.

you could try some length, you said. we'll put in extensions.
i thought about it but declined.
i only want to use what's mine, i said.

a bird in the hand: I wrote a recipe for my Black father, but i never tasted it. i felt like a thief whenever i took in the smells from any kitchen at all.

i washed and detangled the day before but didn't straighten. just blow it straight before you come, you said. i didn't.

two birds with one stone: story is hair is story is hair is story. there are poems in my hair, and i want to know what they are. i want to take this stone out of my lap and carry it gracefully on my head like my African ancestors. i want you to make these braids so tight that i never lose my balance again. the headache is the weight of it all.

i practice flying with this weight that you have carried your whole life. i could fly without it but i would be a lesser bird. until i can carry all of me,

i will always fall.

bird's nest: a place of rest for a bird who has spent all day flying. a sanctuary.

a Home.

star/light/tours

star/light/star
po/lice/car
find/an/in/jun/man
(   )
star/light/star
drive/him/far
far/out/as/you/can
(   )
star/light/bright
dar/rell/night
walk/ing/back/through/snow
(   )
star/light/bright
live/and/fight
moon/a/bove/you/glows
(   )
star/light/field
child/named/neil
one/shoe/on/his/feet
(   )
star/light/field
night/can/feel
fro/zen/hearts/that/beat
(   )
star/light/road
night/is/cold
walk/ing/till/he's/numb
(   )
star/light/road
bears/the/load
fath/ers/sis/ters/sons
(   )
star/light/truth
sits/in/booth
swear/ing/on/their/god

(   )
star/light/truth
nail/and/tooth
all/-white/ju/ry/nods
(   )
star/light/fight
won/by/night
can/not/raise/the/dead
(   )
star/light/fight
can/dle/light
when/the/ver/dict's/read
(   )
star/light/score
val/d'/or
jer/ry/tells/his/sto/ry
(   )
star/light/score
ma/ny/more
cops/make/jer/ry/sor/ry
(   )
star/light/pretty
ma/ny/cities
keep/the/sto/ry/small
(   )
star/light/pretty
ed/it/wiki
star/light/saw/it/all
(   )
star/light/moon
sas/ka/toon
tries/to/soothe/the/sting
(   )
star/light/moon
bright/as/noon
wat/ches/ev'/ry/thing
(

this page is blank for neilstonechild. the following page is blank for the many men and women who are victims or survivors of canada's starlight tours.

built on bones

1   bones call ta blood/blood calls ta bone

                                              land an
                                               sea an
                                                  sky
                                         carry   the
                                              messages

when ah   close ma ee's   an lie   very stell

                              ma blood   turns   an

                   churns   feverboil

ma ears hold haunting
wind-songchoir-cries
of ma people,   long buried.

clerrances created a

          d   i   a   s   -

                p   o   r   a   ;

                    kelled most shipped sum med way
                                        fer the all-

imp-
ortant
                    british…   …   … sheep.

oor elders say yoor lairds / came like the bonxie.
those who did not / leave our ayland withtherheids

        doon were evacuated / thas a nice word

for wit you used

      the women for, and sum o the men
          couldna be used.

yoor redcoats took / ootoor chiefs / calledus savages. you

made it illegal ta speak
or ta
              wear oor own clothes. / small-pox an big-
                slaughter, you hunted / the rest of us

                          doon

        sharp beaks an all.

we returned word-
less naked bloody chained

2   *resistance* formed maerlyfutsteps

as we refused yoor
peachy pastoral
kindnesses och
an piss on ye.

uncivilized you said.
who will teach
the cheldren?
that is wit ah want

to know. all oor
teachings and oor
language and oor
kenship tees ware lost

ta the travesty of
education and that
pitchfork reledgion.
you want me ta

comb ma hair.
what is wild?
hooses of stone
carriers of culture

long lost, we stayed
blood an bone
undistarbed. noo, we
hoose the collection

living museums
the bone smoke
brengs us stories
stone an wind an

tweed an tongue -
the homeland in oor
chest an belly.
don touch.

3   tertle

isthe   ayland

               biggest

                                       ayland

                                                  a
                                                  h

                                                  h
                                                  a
                                                  v
                                                  e

                                                  e
                                                  v
                                                  e
                                                  r

                                                  s
                                                  e
                                                  e
                                                  n
                                                  .

&hoomeny museums do ye have here?

&hoomeny schools did ye build on their ancestors?
                    on thare old women anthare young men?

&do you feel the blood fever?

&do you boil at the see-ght of buildings on bone?

&can you breng them Home?

&will they wear the skens an speak the tongues they remember?

&when will the dead tell their own stories?

    treaties of bone and blood need no
                                signature.

    (another continentbuilt on bones anscreaming fer blood.)

listen!!!!!!!!!!!

reet-nooooruniversities store their ancestors

                                                                     i
                                                                     n

                                                                     c
                                                                     a
                                                                     r
                                                                     d
                                                                     b
                                                                     o
                                                                     a
                                                                     r
                                                                     d

                                                                     b
                                                                     o
                                                                     x
                                                                     e
                                                                     s
                                                                     .

did ye really think that
we, in oor pain
could be

                                            guilt   less

??????????

                                          och

        blood is hot

        bones is sharp

                                                                ah said

don
                    feckin

                                                                  touch.

a true story of 2 suicidal men

                                              in scar-borough

my brother is the colour of the cream-er
in my neighbour's instant coffee. when he
grabbed for the gun right off of a white cop
in a parking lot in scarborough, he hoped

                      to be shot - but ended up getting hugged.

my neighbour is the colour of the rust
on my brother's silver spoon. when he
phoned 911 for crisis right from his car
in the very same parking lot, he   hoped

                      to be hugged - but ended up getting shot.

      we called him blingy and the papers never printed his name

indiginnocent (for donaldmarshall jr.)

junior was a firecracker
running through the town
never took a [threat] or [insult]
lying on the ground
he was next to be a leader
raised his whisper to a shout
said, "three more months, and i
can vote this [f*cker] out!"

junior knew sandy from
around down here
often shared a smoke
and a joke and a beer
junior didn't [kill] him but
he couldn't get an ear
sitting there in [prison] for
eleven long years

on the way home now
his dad says, "buckle up"
junior's [confused], he missed
the memo on that stuff
his mama [cries], his sister says
"hey, this you've gotta see
they don't use records no more
this here is a cd"

junior got acquitted
but the [bad rap] stuck
[court] said he was the author of
his own [bad luck]
they'd see him ten years later on
antlered as a buck
they didn't raise junior but
he sure as hell grew up

donald survived prison but his time there shortened his life. he passed in 2009.

high as home,

        selling our souls to buy

b
e
l
o
n
g
i
n
g

hey, hey,
        you look like you come from
            nowhere, nowhere good, nowhere that
wants ya. come in, come in. the party's
        just startin'. your pain's just about to
end.

hey, hey,
        you look like you need to
            forget, forget everything, everything
            they
did to ya. siddown, siddown. the good shit
        just got here. it's cool, we'll teach ya
how.

hey, hey,
        didn't your mama never tell ya
            nice, nice folks do drugs? nice folks
lookin' for nice folks. like you, like you. not all
good but not
        all bad neither, i'll bet. who else you
got to trust?
                    trust me.

sometimes ,

>when i scream ,every sound in the worldfrees itself from deep inside my chestand i become a stronger vesselcontainingall of the screamsof every woman, everywhere, from every time ,all of their voices burstingthrough me , firing from behind my ribcagefrom a passage that leads everywhere , reverberating throughout my body , echoing in time and place ,
>*screaming* , screaming

island tongue

in the schoolyard, you ask me boldly   (but not unkindly)
like maybe you reallywanna know.

                    you ask: you speakin' een-glesh?

no, i say quick, then alsoquickquicki
change my mind.

well, yes, i mean, in a way.
we don use their inglish but

it's easier, see   ? it's enn-ga-leeshwithout
the red tapethe locked doorthe years of
sense-a-less rules and con   trol

it's inna-glishh almost, but for freeer people
who wurk reel dayssleep good at nite got no time to waist on
rules an rules anexsepshuns to rules an

reggalayshuns and conjugayshuns and stippalayshuns

fa peepl who be as common as cents.
see like this here - and i show you.

                        oh! its like patois, you say.

likewut now   ?

                            and you show me.

ah!i can feel

yorinng-lich. lykfoaksmaykin
      songs frum werdswerdsfrum scentssense frum meenin
          werds da peent peechassungs da onsakweschuns

                                        yai got kewschuns man

dun we all.

                    anstarries, starrys. yesssss.ifeeeeeel u.

trubble is, wunce u lerndeyrools
u canna eva go bak 2 beinfuh-ree

                    wuns u loozyaaksentyalooz da kee
                yalooz da senns of it oll. 4eva na, yutrapd
                innasortafoyay in between insyd an awtsyd

riteritean u dun hav a lang-wich or a tung
ya tung jus flowtslyk da eye land it left

                        yalefyaaylan 2 hey ayland gurl

hay we
floawtinflawwtinflowwwwwwwtinnnnnnnnnnnnnnnn.

so u n i find uthaz who is awt der floatin an we colls out:

      "   tell me a-boat yoraylind-ayland tung!yesss
    tel me haw ur antees bakhowm laff at ur ka-nay-jun tung
       anya klass-maits laff at ya bak-hoam tung and
        u arntsher if u gots 2 tungs o nun. girl
    tell me ollya sta-reez, tel me in a lang-a-wich dat maiks
                kommunsents!   "

songs for [caged] birds   (for angela   cardinal)

        standing in [shackles], miss cardinal sings
telling the [courtroom] of [terrible things]
        her face full of [bruises], her back sprouting wings
standing in [shackles], miss cardinal sings

        back from the [courthouse], miss cardinal flies
in the back of the wagon, no [tears] touch her eyes
        the girl and her [rapist] are [cuffed] side by side
back from the [courthouse], miss cardinal flies

        [accused] of no [crime], yet miss cardinal stays
[locked up] in remand for five [grueling days]
        singing her story, her dark eyes ablaze
[accused] of no [crime], yet miss cardinal stays

        several months later, miss cardinal [died]
the artist and poet whom [justice denied]
        she spoke of her innocence, earned all her pride
several months later, miss cardinal [died]

        now bright as a spirit, miss cardinal soars
[injustice] and [lies] will affect her no more
        her song is for peace and her song is for [war]
now bright as a spirit, miss cardinal soars   [.]

please find out what other injustices angela faced and what she liked to do in her spare time before she was murdered -

family portrait

when visitors say it is a nice portrait of the four of us
i say five of us. there are five.

the father is the negative space, please see
the careful way he winds himself distantly around our four
bodies

see how the father is more present in his absence, squint
and let the background breathe solid sentience, see how much

more grief, more space, more of everything
he has become, see how

the photographer uses negative space so effectively,
how they drown their subject in nothingness, yes,

what an artist, to capture such a bold composition,
to call it a family portrait, to frame it, to sell it back to me,

to smile at the small face on the left surrounded by
three small children and a thick, white grief

and charge it for the session, for the photos, for existing
in a negative space that can only be staved off by

the flash of a camera and the fervent hope
that no one who ever sees this photo will be an art critic

the gardener

    the roses know her   other   name

        (though she smells less   sweet).

the soil stains on her glittering palmsand clay-coloured
    tan on her neck

inevitably fffaaaddd   when the thorns and sticks

are all that survive the malignant tendrils and frosty sabo-tage of december, yet,

                              they swiftly return with the
        sensualsoundsofsummer'shedonistic*hums*-and-*sighs*.

when it is   time to return the   anxious callusesand
    homeless blisters

to her   strong, itching fingers

she clutches (a new trowel) and plunges(into foliage) that

        boasts bolder coloursthan the season before.

she can scarcely   believe   (she has not forgotten)
  ,

though all these years have passed ,

        the

    songs she always sang to the noonday sun   .

you think autistic people cannot be journalists because we suffer from black-and-white thinking

- and it just so happens that

greyscale, too, is a spectrum: how black, how white,

how colourless would you like my kind to appear when we are flattened under your palms

and what if i, dead, am still a mess? do you see?

she don't bite, my father said about me as a child.

what he meant was

it ain't her fault if your black-or-white skin reacts to her saliva. it was, though

if you actually think we're all in this together, but i

wasn't the one with

black-and-white thinking

if you think black-and-white is a metaphor.

shall i compound the issue, yes, it's a pun,
kaleidoscopically

because i have cried
watching a mosquito draw first blood

      prayerful that her larvae will thrive on
neurodivergency

    just as i have killed others without mercy,
staining the wallpaper in my kitchen

  with my children's mixed blood. and it was not murder

and it was

yes, it all depended on everything, everything

         and every news outlet
     can paint with blood too.

     but my brain, my brain, so beautiful

  in nuance, listens for wings

little blue blanket (after ritahester)

when i was born they wrapped me
in my burial shroud.

and i have been a pall-bearer for ideas
fragile fetty in the veins of the dis-eased

who wake up from the amurican dream
to find they was not asleep at all

oh, but i want to be covered in bees.
i want to lick the danger until it quivers

dirty and dis-illusioned and wrapped in
the patchwork of some-one warm and sane

the subject, my-self, the object, danger;
the subject, some-one, the object, a quilt.

yes, i understand the desire to live
in a tent on the lawn of the elite, unblank-eted

but i swaddled my-self in some-thing so much bigger.
they'll bury me in tech-nicolour one day.

i want to piss blood in the street
and run from the en-raged, re-leasing

the blue fabric into the sky, no longer
a noose around my neck, it flies, and me,

at the top of my ever-loving lungs, scream-ing,
"who cares, who cares, who cares!!!"

if you don't know who rita was, you should. please sit here in this white space and find out.

the ballad of mrs. g   (for donna george)

a lovely girl of six-teen years
with belly full of child
prepares to leave the life she [fears]
of [men], and parties wild
forgetting [things] she can't unsee
and strength she hasn't needed
young mrs. g goes on to be

> a woman, undefeated
> a woman, undefeated

yes, mrs. g, adam, and three

> young children, whom God treated
> all children, whom God treated.

another year, another child
another time, [detained]
another pregnancy that ends
in [tears], her name [defamed]
the second babe they also [took]
the [drugs] become a friend
as angels name her in their book

> and swear a happy end
> and swear a happy end

a[system] launched a [mean right hook]

> her heart still yet to mend,
> her heart still yet to mend.

the third child too, is taken now
but mrs.g has grown
an adult now, she wonders how
to outgrow this alone
and if i too, by [sniffing glue]
could be made to forget
three babies who, though i loved true,

        i'd hardly even met
        i'd hardly even met

yes, then i, too, i tell you true

        would take [drugs] to forget,
        would take [drugs] to forget.

child number four, and there's a [score]
to settle, bit by bit
those who are [poor], they [target] more
and mrs.g can't quit
the [[[cfs]]], claiming their best
keep [permanent black files]
the [feds] suggest it's for the best

        that she [abort] the child
        that she [abort] the child

but, feeling blessed, she'll do no less

        than let her babe run wild,
        she'll let her babe run wild.

now mrs.g, choosing to see
her whole pregnancy through
yearns still to be a mother, free
and hide until she's due
although she's grown, and lives alone,
the [judge] sees fit to [order]
her to [disown] her will. his tone

        shows nothing warm towards her
        shows nothing warm towards her

until [his verdict]'s overthrown

        they'll [cuff] her and [transport] her,
        they'll [cuff] her and [transport] her.

        (so says the [news reporter],
        so says the [news reporter].)

[alone] that night, [locked] in a room
she bends to say a prayer
and in the [darkness] of the [gloom]
she feels there's someone there
a gentle reassurance rests
the cravings all have gone
and by the time the supreme court

        rules the first [judge] was wrong
        rules the first [judge] was wrong

she holds her baby to her breast

        a little boy, so strong,
        a little boy, so strong.

have you   ?

have you felt
just   outside   the city
smells of   sage and   ceremonial fire
d riftinga   cross thetra -
cksthat div/ide
your heart   ?

have you   *heard*
at the   *edge*
of the trees, tipp *ing*
like a turkey   *vulture*
the first drum   *beats*
of boys who   *want*
to be   *men*   ?

have you seen
at the river's beeeeeend
while step-ping naked
from your   brand-name
clothes, a cheek-y spirit
mov-ing quickly
on the   bank   ?

have you tried
at the age where
c-o-n-n-e-c-t-i-o-n happens   ,
as the salmon !know!
how to go Home   ,
to braid your
foreign hair   ?   have you   ?

52

full circle

when i was born, it rained.(   )

my father does not remember (   ) this.

                    he did not stay to see the flowers.

when my first child was born, it did not rain.(   )

i do not remember (   ) this either.

                        it might not be true.

diving devilishly from telephone wires into sunset-coloured valleys

the falcon fishes fast and freely until ice forms,

              freez-ing(   ) time.

and i did not braid my daughter's hair until she (   ) aged

until she could begin to understand the plight (   )

                  of her grandfather's people.

my sons' hair i cut right away, and then every three moons, again.

a child of mixed blood, i did not feel (   )

                                      worthy to raise warriors.

the moon does not worry about whether (or not) she will be luminous

when she rises over alkebu-lan, over aotearoa,

                                    over mishiikenhminissi.

depending on the clouds, on the night, on the perspective of the observer   ,

the moon is not necessarily brighter when she has come

                                          (full circle).

white knuckles/blacklists

when george couldn't breathe,   ,
         i was writing a shopping list, and i wasn't   afraid
of dying, and i was watching   him   ,   choked

when george couldn't breathe,   ,
         mascara fell in heavy   drops all over. black
on my hand and fingers. black on my shopping list

when george couldn't breathe,
         rivers of   black marched over my knuckles;
rivers of   Black marched through the streets

         knuckles of all colours

                    in
                         the
                              air

when george couldn't breathe,
         my shopping list lay neglected while iheldmybreath
         ,
coveredmymouth   , knuckles   white in
         horror

whengeorgecouldn'tbreathe,   *neither could i*

         but the difference is: my light/skinned ass is still
                         alive

to cry and ask why and go buy my groceries

please exist in this white space for george, and all our BIPOC men who cannot breathe in white spaces

driving

        my   father used to drive a car.
a little grey mazda, because his   father said
mazdas are the way to go, and children become
     their   fathers, at least for a time. the car had
go-fast stripes, red and orange, but my   dad didn't
go fast. lights, red and blue tailed him even
     when he drove so slow my   mother called him magoo.
          i clutched my   sister's small hand through
    the   baby's carseat handle even though   we knew
     dad hadn't done anything wrong.   we sat straight
when thewaist of a [cop] appeared through the window,
              squeezed when the knock came,
        smiled when the moonface
  asked   daddy what he was doing off the reservation
                                    today
and if he had had anything to drink and then
    if he had a gun, while the [cop] fingered his own gun,
  and   i felt thesum of two hatreds bubble as my
              father

mumbled his apologies as if he was ducking a whip, and i
hated the [[white whip-wielder]] but also my   father
    because in his desperation to keep us
        safe he seemed like a coward
                and i never once hated
        my   mother even though she laughed
because   indians were always the butts of jokes and
    their   children were supposed to be seen
        and not heard and
    we were too used to exercising our right to remain

   [silent].

red herring

i am the hybrid daughter of an immigrant and a whore
i was born with the desire to get more.
i was born to save myself. to score
a point with god a point with the devil
a line into my flesh, pawn that *i am*.
sometimes, you know, i pretend to play for the right team
white-on-sunday came off in the shower
black at drugstore is a secret shopper that never comes off
just follows me everywhere
until i walk the aisles with twenties visible in my hand

i am a red herring
i am not the thing
you think *i am*
and *i was* born to get more.

i come to canada on a boat.
my mother pays our passage with her curves
sailors sliding into her dips and divots, swerves
avoiding anything that serves my memory

and her memories are buried under so many layers of meth and mania, yes,

women never get what they deserve.

do not see the overdotted map that is my sperm donor.

he came in my mother and went.

see the queer hero, the brave man who in 1992 denies himself and marries my mother

    the only man *i will* ever call my father.

    hides from his own mother's shame standing inside my mother's femininity.

    at least she is just a whore and not a man, his mother nods,

    thanking god that conversion therapy works as she crosses her chest

    and my mother's mother mutters how blessed, how blessed. my grandchild will be canadian now.

    a perfect union, yes?

my father takes me on their honeymoon with them

neither of them touches the other

but in the photographs *i am* in the sweetheart suite hot tub surrounded by balloons

eating chocolate with both my hands.

i imagine my parents rest.

i imagine this is when their hearts first make plans

to blame me for their disappointments. but

i am the red herring

i am not the thing

they think *i am*.

i was born to get more,

the daughter of a closeted gay man and a woman of the night

                i know how to avoid a fight.

          i learned the arts of invisibility and diversion

           i know how to throw you off my trail. yes

  i learned to lose my voice, to let another make my choices for me, to die in the name of safety.

it takes them until age sixty to file for divorce.

my grandparents are dead and they have run out of boomers to perform for.

i stand, chocolate in both my hands, and watch.

age 61, my father learns his language for the first time, whispers

makademaashkikiwaboo as he stirs his coffee in a little cafe on church street *he buys* purple skinny jeans and hangs a pride flag on his apartment door

he is born to be more

        and my mother drowns in the water we crossed over in.

                crosses her chest and chokes on shame

      the feeling that *she was* good enough for every man but him

           and *i am* the hybrid child of freedom and shame

              there are days when*i can* barely speak my name

                  when *i would* die to break my chains

           when *i could* step off the boat out of the tub out of the drugstore out of my skin but

i am a red herring

a hybrid home of suffering

seeking to fling my slippery body back into the sea

and *he is* not the thing she thinks and*she is* not the thing he thinks and*i am* not the thing they think*i am*.

            i was born with the desire to be more than he or she

                      a mystery that isn't me.

red herring in the sea   *i'm*free.

                                      i'm free.

aftermath

when our worlds burned
our hearts became wax
drooling, pooling,
cooling and encasing us
in hardened shells as smooth as teeth
our scalding skin unsoothed beneath.
how will we survive the aftermath
if we don't cccrack our hearts open?
how will we   breathe   if we don't burst
?

blindness

don't go, is what i say to the mirror;

    is what i spent my life saying.

        take these parts of me and make them two-
dim/ens/ion/al. take them and

turn them into something only perceived;

    into pages in a book

        (.laerenoynaotsdrawkcabraeppalliw taht)
reflect my stories until, until, until.

don't go. these stubborn snatches of story that want to be told

        come   free

    with a humiliating slowness as i strain to remember in

        3/dim/ens/ion/zzz

(or maybe 4, where i travel through time just to see what i'd look like in a   world before mirrors. or 5, where there's no such thing as memories because)

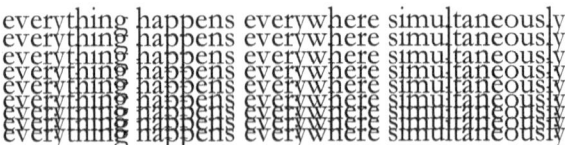

in every timeline, if you snort too much coke off a mirror, you'll go blind, or some shit like that.

      or maybe it's that woman with the snakes for hair that i should never have fallen for or that time i looked at the sun because nobody stopped me or the fact that i know i

    shouldn't have been going to damascus alone in

              the first place.

it doesn't matter:

in every timeline, the blindness is my fault.

        trauma has painted a blank canvas all over every

        colour   in the   world

          i have forgotten what colour is

and how to describe colour to someone as blind as your own reflection?

          and i got another question, man

if a person loses their vision in childhood and learns language with sight as input but then loses their memories of having seen to injury or disease, does their language make sense anymore   ?

    they can speak to you, a see-ing person, and you will under-stand, but from their new perspective,

they will only be describing an un-reality, a land-scape and a time-line that are i-rrelevant and de-void of attach-ment to any-thing that can be felt or un-derstood.

you can only place their time-worn fing-ers on a knife and say,

        see, pain.

or uncurl your tongue against their soft lips and say,

        see, pleasure.

the person will say, yes, i see, but they will not see at all.

this is all hypothetical, of course.

this is all rhetorical, of course.

of course.

i look in the mirror and   see. a thread dangles tantalizingly from your waist. i pull on the thread but only snatches come through, fluffy and tapered, each more frayed than the last.

see? this is why i don't wear sweaters.

see? this is why i don't keep mirrors.

see?

                                      see?

sssse   e   e   e

                   e   e

     e

              ?

                                  s
                           e

e
?

see?

see?

Acknowledgements

I wanted to use Arlene Joseph's wise words about community to thank you all for this book coming to be, but I didn't get the rights in time. So instead, just know: I listen to people when they eat my fry bread.

About the Author

Murgatroyd Monaghan is an Autistic mother, writer, spoken word artist and poet of mixed descent. Her spoken word won first place at the Wordstock Sudbury Literary Festival and Myths and Mirrors.

Her piece "Thumbs" won the Pacific Spirit Poetry Prize. She has been a finalist for dozens of national literary prizes including the Room Poetry Contest and the CBC Nonfiction Prize. Other writing has been published in Chapter House Review, PRISM, and the Humber Literary Review, among many others.

Murgatroyd has devoted her adult life to motherhood and is pursuing writing now that her children are older. She is working on several book-length projects. A former asylum-seeker, Monaghan was raised in Ontario, Canada.

Also by Murgatroyd Monaghan

For Soldiers and Sailors Alike

Carefully crafted to be both a requiem for and a celebration of the unique gifts and injuries of womanhood, For Soldiers and Sailors Alike is requisite poetry for our modern world. Murgatroyd Monaghan walks hand in hand with readers as they embark on a tour of combat that is at times painful, at times beautiful, and yet always hauntingly familiar. Using both traditional and contemporary forms of poetry, Monaghan opens readers' wounds alongside her own and then sews them back together again, ultimately stitching a literary patchwork that is as diverse and united as women are themselves. Each poem is a voice that refuses to relent, despite battlefields and oceans, as it decorates women for their unique forms of bravery. In the pages of this book, readers of all genders, backgrounds, and ages will be inspired to reclaim and view their own personal story in a more empowering way than they have ever been guided to see it before.

More Books from Off Topic Publishing

All titles available at

offtopicpublishing.com/shop

or from your usual book and ebook vendors

All Forgotten Now, by Jennifer Mariani

In these poems, Jennifer Mariani grieves a life she can't return to, as she struggles to belong elsewhere. This work explores the reality of growing up white in post-independence Zimbabwe: Jennifer's own privilege juxtaposed with everyday poverty and racism. The poems in this book cry out with grief and rage and loss, and sometimes celebration. Every page is warm with the heat of Africa and wet with the tears of unbelonging.

"[A] stirring collection."

– Yejide Kilanko, bestselling author of *Daughters Who Walk This Path* and *A Good Name*

Wayward & Upward: Stories & Poems

A woman runs from a cult leader.

A man watches a crowd carry a baby into the woods.

A boy makes a childhood friend who is much older than she appears.

The forty pieces in this book unite two creative endeavours at the heart of humanity: making music and telling stories.

"Metafictional conversations and stand-alone pieces alike shine with creativity, taking thought experiments to a whole other level of engagement."

– Michelle Butler Hallett, Winner of the Thomas Raddall Atlantic Fiction Prize, *Constant Nobody*

Wanderers:
Poems From Those Who Cross Borders

Whether seeking asylum, travelling between homes, or studying abroad, these poems shimmer and roar with the chaos, beauty and astonishment that come with crossing borders. The impetus for crossing varies, but whatever the reason, borders loom large in the lives of these poets.

"Everyone's experience of borders is different, and beautiful. Read this book."

– Mary Grace van der Kroef, author of *The Branch That I Am*

Exhaustion: Limited Reserves

Used up or worn out. Reaching the limits of our personal and collective resources. Laying waste to the planet. Burning fuel until there's nothing left but fumes. Each story and poem in this book engages exhaustion anew, revealing human struggles, moments of grace, and a relentless questioning.

"Society pressures us to carry stress, even when it weighs more than we do. These pieces reflect that common experience and give words to the silent struggles that isolate us within ourselves."

– Renee Cronley, nurse and author of *Burnout*

Home: An Anthology

What is home? Is it a place? A feeling? A person? Does it shift and change? Can you point towards it but never quite attain it? Through poems and flash fiction from diverse voices, this anthology wrestles with the complexities of belonging.

"The voice came again. 'You are welcome here, Jia, if you are as committed to peace as you claim. Come and take refuge.'"
 – from "Refuge" by Dawn Vogel (short story in *Home*)

Standing Up: A Charity Anthology for Ukraine

You rose up: against tyranny, convention, rudeness, unfavourable odds, malevolence, apathy. Against your boss, your barista, your worst enemy, your best friend, yourself. You saved the day. Actually, maybe made things worse. Made a difference. Got flattened. Did it work? Well, life's complicated. But one thing's for sure: On that day, you saw something you believed was wrong and you took action.

This anthology's proceeds will be 100% donated to the Canada-Ukraine Foundation.

The Price of Cookies, by Finnian Burnett

Two brothers face their mother's impending death. A convenience store clerk balances compassion with duty. A grieving soldier receives a package of cookies meant for someone else. In this series of connected flash fiction pieces, people navigate the trials of life with tears, arguments and, above all, love and compassion.

"Lives interwoven and cookies that arrive too late. This bravura collection of linked stories provides a profound lesson in empathy, of pouring yourself into someone else's life, someone else's pain, to see it from the inside, looking out."

– Will Ferguson, Giller Prize-winning author of *419*

www.ingramcontent.com/pod-product-compliance
Lightning Source LLC
Chambersburg PA
CBHW020544080526
44583CB00013B/992